Original title:
Jests in the Juniper Grove

Copyright © 2025 Creative Arts Management OÜ
All rights reserved.

Author: Amelia Montgomery
ISBN HARDBACK: 978-1-80567-415-3
ISBN PAPERBACK: 978-1-80567-714-7

Echoes of Ecstasy in the Clever Canopy

Beneath the boughs where shadows play,
A squirrel in shades of bright array,
Dances with nuts, oh what a sight,
While friends all giggle in pure delight.

The owl wears glasses, thinks he's wise,
But trips on twigs in his own surprise,
The rabbits snicker, it's quite a scene,
As he stumbles through brush, so clumsy and keen.

The breeze whispers secrets, just for fun,
A breeze that twirls 'round each little one,
Tickles the leaves, they rustle and tease,
As critters conspire with laughter to please.

At dusk, the fireflies put on a show,
Winking and blinking like stars in a row,
Chasing each other in gleeful delight,
Illuminating the giggles of night.

So gather 'neath branches, where whimsy blooms,
Where laughter and joy conquer gloomy presumes,
In this clever canopy of chuckles and cheer,
Life's little wonders bring all of us near.

Puns of the Petite Passages

In the tiny nooks, laughter springs,
A squirrel stumbles, it's got two wings!
With acorns flying, oh what a sight,
Chasing its tail, in a whirlwind flight.

Tickling branches giggle in cheer,
A chipmunk whispers, "Pass me a beer!"
With every pun, the leaves seem to sway,
As nature joins in on this silly play.

Satirical Shadows in the Forest's Heart

Through twisted roots, shadows parade,
A wise old owl gives a charade.
"Why did the rabbit cross the path?
To escape the fox's witty wrath!"

A raccoon in a mask, so sly,
Claims he's just dressing for a pie.
With every joke, the trunk trees creak,
As sunlight sends giggles, far from bleak.

Tales of Jest Under the Age-Old Boughs

Beneath the branches, stories unfold,
A weary tortoise sings brave and bold.
"Slow and steady wins the race," he grins,
While the hare looks back and softly spins.

A fox with charm and a wink so sly,
Claims to build dreams that touch the sky.
With each tall tale, the wind does tease,
Bringing chuckles among the trees.

Breezy Banter Among Ferns

Ferns exchange whispers, secrets they share,
A bee buzzes by, as if unaware.
"What's the best nectar?" the flowers ask,
"Just sip from life, it's the sweetest task!"

With breezy laughter, the meadow spins,
Where every blossom plays along with grins.
As nature chuckles, the world feels light,
In this playful dance, all things feel right.

Enigmas of Ecstasy in the Groves

In shadows where the whispers play,
A tickle of breeze brings joy to stay.
Squirrels dance in acorn delight,
Chasing tales till the fall of night.

A gnome with a grin, peeks from the moss,
Sharing riddles he hears from the grass.
The owls hoot back with an echoing cheer,
As laughter weaves magic, bright and clear.

The leaves giggle softly in a sunbeam's glow,
While shadows perform in a comical show.
Bumbling bees buzz with a flirty intent,
In this groovy, playful establishment.

So gather ye round, let your spirits soar,
In this grove of glee, there's always more.
With each chuckle that breezes through,
Life's little enigmas become fresh and new.

A Symphony of Smiles in the Forest

In woodland lanes where chuckles sprout,
A symphony of smiles dances about.
The trees bend low, exchanging winks,
As leaves skip along, without any links.

A rabbit wore glasses, quite debonair,
While squirrels debated who'd won the fair.
An orchestra of giggles rings out loud,
Resounding joy, weaving through the crowd.

The sun flirts playfully with the flocks,
Birds chatter tales from unique blocks.
Marshmallow clouds on a cotton-candy sky,
Invite the laughter, lifting spirits high.

So let us all sway to this pleasant sound,
In a forest where laughter knows no bound.
For in each note, a story unfolds,
As smiles gather warmth in the sunlit molds.

The Lure of Laughter in the Leafy Domain

Where roots intertwine in the merry ground,
Laughter lures souls that seek joy unbound.
A caterpillar dances, shaking its tail,
As fireflies glow, illuminating the trail.

The brook bubbles on with giggles and glee,
Telling secrets to each thirsty tree.
Mushrooms wear hats, as they gather round,
In this leafy domain, mirth can be found.

The breeze carries tales from the soft ferns,
Each whisper a jest, each chuckle, it turns.
Sassy critters with splendid flair,
Join in the revels without a care.

So stroll through the leaves where delight grows wide,
In the laughter-filled corners, so proudly abide.
For in every hollow, and under each beam,
Life's merry symphony flows like a dream.

Echoed Giggles in Nature's Gallery

In Nature's gallery where colors burst,
Echoes of giggles, we quench our thirst.
A fox with a flourish, prances with grace,
While clouds join the fun, spinning, they chase.

A beaver in glasses, studying the scene,
Winks at the daisies, so bright and keen.
Each chuckle resonating, a tuning fork,
As shadows embark on a playful corkscrew walk.

The daisies all giggle, swaying in glee,
As the wind tells the tale of an old, wise bee.
With every rustle, a story is spun,
This canvas of laughter is never quite done.

So come take a peek at this whimsical show,
With echoes of joy in a vibrant flow.
In Nature's embrace, where laughter abides,
Find beauty in giggles, where the heart confides.

Kites and Kinks in the Leafy Labyrinth

In the breeze, kites twist and turn,
Strings tangled tight, oh how they yearn.
Laughter echoes in the trees,
As squirrels dance with the gentle breeze.

Bouncing balls dodge the shady fronds,
While sunlight plays, creating blond bonds.
Each leaf a stage, each branch a throne,
In this quirky world, we're never alone.

Melodies of Mirth Beneath Verdant Veils

Underneath the canopy, giggles float,
A rabbit dons a new, silly coat.
The frogs croak tunes of carefree cheer,
While everyone joins in, drawing near.

Wind whistles songs through the clover beds,
Ticklish tales that dance in our heads.
Shade and sun take turns in a game,
Where laughter lingers, always the same.

Whispers of Wit in the Greenery

Among the ferns, wisecracks unfold,
A millipede claims it's grown quite bold.
With every twist in the winding path,
The trees join in with a lighthearted laugh.

Butterflies tease the sleepy blooms,
As bees buzz jokes, in sunny rooms.
Each shadow laughs, shimmers in light,
In this grove, everything feels just right.

Intrigue Among the Twisted Roots

Beneath the soil, mischief brews,
With whispers hidden from curious views.
The gnomes play tricks on wandering toes,
While roots intertwine in their wily throws.

Mice play tag in a game of stealth,
Skipping along with delightful health.
Each twist and turn, a riddle to tease,
In this playful world, we feel the ease.

Whispers of the Woodland Wits

Amid the trees, a squirrel grins,
He tells of nuts and playful sins.
With acorns stacked, a tiny throne,
He reigns in laughter, never alone.

A fox in socks, so proud and spry,
He dances under the bright blue sky.
With every leap, he trips and falls,
Yet bounces back, and joy enthralls.

Laughter Beneath the Canopy

The owls hoot jokes in the cool, night air,
While rabbits chuckle without a care.
A badger tells tales of the days gone by,
With giggles and snorts that make all sigh.

The breeze plays tricks, a tickling tease,
Rustling leaves that dance with ease.
In the shade, shadows play and prance,
Inviting all to join their chance.

The Playful Pines' Tales

Beneath the pines, a party grows,
With frisky fawns and cheerful crows.
They share a game of hide and seek,
With laughter echoing, so unique.

A pouncing pup, with floppy ears,
Chases butterflies, loses his fears.
Round and round, the giggles soar,
In this woodland tale, there's always more.

Secrets of the Sprightly Shrubs

Amongst the vines, a secret's shared,
With whispers soft, none are scared.
The porcupine jokes about his spikes,
While the hedgehog grins, sharing likes.

A chipmunk's dance, with twirls and spins,
Each little step, where laughter begins.
They plan a feast, a berry delight,
Under the moon, until the night.

Secrets of the Hidden Glade

In shadows deep where giggles grow,
The hidden folks put on a show.
With twinkling eyes and mischief bright,
They dance around in pure delight.

A squirrel juggles acorns with flair,
While rabbits hop without a care.
The breeze carries laughter, wild and free,
In this glade of glee, come see, come see!

Echoes of Merriment Under Branches

Beneath the trees where shadows play,
The critters gather, a grand buffet.
They trade tall tales, make big claims,
Of brave adventures and silly games.

An owl with glasses counts the jokes,
While hedgehogs roll with giggling pokes.
The sun winks down, a playful tease,
In this branchy alcove, hearts find ease.

Frolics in the Fragrant Boughs

The blossoms laugh in hues so bright,
As bees buzz round in pure delight.
A fox in boots prances with cheer,
Chasing shadows that disappear.

The lilting breeze brings tunes to dance,
While squirrels join in a merry prance.
Nature's stage, a comic play,
Where every leaf has fun to say.

Chortles in the Shaded Hollow

In the hollow where the sunlight bends,
Creatures gather, they're all good friends.
A badger tells tales of wild heights,
As crickets play their late-night flights.

With hats made of leaves, the band takes flight,
The rabbits hop high, what a sight!
Laughter echoes, a joyous sound,
In this hidden nook, mirth abounds.

Mischief Among the Mossy Roots

Beneath the shade where shadows dance,
A squirrel in shorts does a silly prance.
The mushrooms giggle, round and small,
As bumblebees join in the sprawl.

A hedgehog wears a tiny hat,
While caterpillars laugh and chat.
They spin the tales of silly socks,
And moonlight winks from fuzzy rocks.

A rabbit juggles acorns, woo!
While fungi cheer with a clapping crew.
The roots arise and tap their toes,
To rhythms only nature knows.

In this wild game of mirth and cheer,
The woodland echoes, all can hear.
For laughter spins like autumn leaves,
In their tangled web, the grove believes.

Tales of the Twinkling Treetops

A parrot dons a bright bow tie,
As fireflies twinkle in the sky.
The owls take bets on a silly game,
While branches sway, without a shame.

Squirrels slide down the gnarled bough,
Laughing as they try to vow.
A fox recites a cheeky verse,
While the wind giggles, quite diverse.

The stars above join in the fun,
As raccoons dance till the night is done.
The pinecones roll and tumble bold,
Spinning stories waiting to be told.

In this canopy where antics thrive,
Joyful antics come alive.
With every rustle, giggles soar,
In twinkling realms, who could ask for more?

Frolics in the Foliage

Among the leaves, a party brews,
With frogs in shades of vibrant hues.
They leap in time to nature's beat,
While crickets chirp a rhythmic treat.

A snail spins tales of race and speed,
As fireflies flash, their glow a deed.
The grass bows low, a theater grand,
For every creature in the land.

The petals dance with laughter bright,
As shadows play in the fading light.
A rabbit hops with playful grace,
Bringing smiles to every face.

In this green world, joy unconfined,
Stories entwined and laughter blind.
Every rustle is a jovial tune,
In a leafy embrace beneath the moon.

Revelry of the Evergreen Echoes

In the heart of the forest, whispers call,
With pine-scented winds, the creatures sprawl.
A chipmunk cracks a joke or two,
As the tall trees nod, their laughter true.

A dance parade of ferns and fronds,
Where shadows sway like magical ponds.
The bees don crowns of tiny blooms,
As they buzz along with sunny tunes.

Among the roots, the laughter swells,
With mystery and joyous spells.
The echoes of joy float through the space,
As the night goes on, a warm embrace.

With every chirp and flickering light,
The evergreen realm sparks pure delight.
It's a festival of whimsy, wild and free,
Where the spirit of fun is the glee of the tree.

Mirth in the Meadow's Embrace

In the meadow, laughter rings,
As butterflies dance on gentle wings.
A toad croaks jokes from the shade,
While daisies giggle, unafraid.

A squirrel plays tricks with acorns round,
While rabbits hop, joy unbound.
They tumble in grass, a playful spree,
Sharing secrets with buzzing bees.

When the sun sets low, they still jest,
Creating a cheer that never rests.
With shadows long, their spirits soar,
In the meadow's heart, forevermore.

Folk Songs of the Fumbling Ferns

Amidst the ferns, a tune so sweet,
Fumbling footsteps make the beat.
A hedgehog sings with a silly twirl,
As crickets harmonize in a whirl.

The fronds sway gently, a dance they make,
While mischief brews by the babbling lake.
The nightingale chuckles with every rhyme,
As shadows prance in a lighthearted mime.

Fireflies blink in a whimsical show,
While frogs in boots put on a glow.
The fumbles of ferns, a merry affair,
Chasing laughter through the cool night air.

High Spirits in the Hidden Hollow

In a hollow, bright and free,
Green gnomes giggle beneath a tree.
With hats so tall, they bump and fall,
Creating mischief, one and all.

Watch the owls roll their eyes so wide,
As the gnomes stumble, they can't decide.
With silly hats and crooked grins,
Their high spirits spark joy that spins.

A raccoon joins with a crafty plan,
In a dance-off with the smallest man.
When the moonlight beams, it's a riotous sight,
In the hollow, they laugh through the night.

Amusements Amidst the Aromatic Branches

Beneath the boughs, a funny crew,
Squirrels scamper for a nut or two.
A bear in a tie plays cards with trees,
While wolves hum tunes carried by the breeze.

The pine cones drop like confetti fair,
As laughter echoes through fragrant air.
With every rustle, a chuckle escapes,
As critters plot and devise their capes.

The branches sway, no one is shy,
Under twinkling stars, they reach for the sky.
In this grove of fun and mirth,
Joy spills over, celebrating their worth.

Variations of Joy in the Woodland Carpet

In a patch of green, a squirrel taps,
Chasing its own tail, it sometimes flaps.
A rabbit grins wide with an acorn hat,
While a lazy frog sings, 'Just where I sat.'

Leaves whisper tales of the best-seen stunts,
Branches shake laughter, as nature confronts.
The flowers chuckle, with petals aglow,
While twirling around in a breezy show.

A wise old owl hoots, 'The night's ours to claim!'
While fireflies flicker, like stars in a game.
With every funny face that the beetles make,
Even the shadows can't help but shake.

From sunlit pathways to the cool earth's floor,
Joy bounces like balls, always begging for more.
In each corner hidden, mirth waits with glee,
In this woodland carpet, where all must agree.

Serendipity in the Garden of Shadows

In the shade of leaves where giggles hide,
A cat naps, dreaming of a fun-filled ride.
A hedgehog rolls by with a prickle of flair,
As butterflies tease without any care.

The sun peeks through, tickling grass ends,
While playful ants plan their merry weekends.
The lilacs burst forth with a splash of delight,
And the shadows join in for a dance in the night.

A fox prances in with a well-timed jest,
Challenging a turtle to a roaring quest.
While crickets chirp as the laughter grows,
In this garden of shadows, anything goes.

Each bud holds a secret, a giggle, a cheer,
In this sneaky hideaway, all gathers near.
From sprightful whispers to gentle sighs,
Nature's own comedy under the skies.

Lively Laughs in Nature's Embrace

Under the boughs where whispers creep,
Squirrels play peek-a-boo without a peep.
The daisies chuckle, their yellow heads nod,
As a wandering breeze gives a playful prod.

A snail tells tales with a slimy grin,
While the sunflowers dance, trying to spin.
Toads strike poses in the muddy patch,
As laughter erupts in a jovial catch.

The brook purls jokes as it bubbles along,
And the thrush sings high in a comical song.
In nature's embrace, cheer fills the air,
Each rustling leaf holds a prank to share.

As shadows widen in the playful dusk,
And cricket chirps rise like an evening husk,
In every nook, there's a chortle in store,
With lively laughs ringing forevermore!

Joyful Journeys Through Foliage

Through the woods we wander, with wild, bright eyes,
Chasing down echoes of giggles and sighs.
The trees shake their branches, a silly parade,
While mushrooms huddle close, in the sun's soft shade.

A fox ties a ribbon, hatching a scheme,
As butterflies flutter in a whimsical dream.
With every step taken, new fun to be found,
In this laughter-filled journey, our hearts leap and bound.

A tumbling tumbleweed spins, out of control,
While all of creation joins in on the roll.
With every leaf swirling, a dance in the air,
In joyful journeys, nothing's too rare.

The sky winks down, as the day slips away,
With a promise that laughter will always stay.
In the foliage's charm, our spirits take flight,
On this path of delight, where joy feels just right.

Mischievous Muse of the Woodland

In the thicket, laughter flies,
Squirrels dance 'neath vibrant skies.
A fox in shades, a prankster's style,
Steals the grapes, grins all the while.

A whisper here and a giggle there,
Frogs in top hats, oh what a flare!
The owls hoot jokes, outlandish and bright,
As night wraps the trees in soft twilight.

Branches sway with a cheeky tease,
Every rustle invites a sneeze.
In this woodland, glee takes flight,
Where mischief reigns, hearts feel light.

So join the frolic, leave cares behind,
Embrace the fun, you'll surely find.
Nature's jesters play their role,
Mischievous muse of the woodland soul.

Tickling the Treetops at Dusk

As shadows blend at day's soft end,
The breezes play, like a child's friend.
Budding leaves giggle in the air,
While crickets strum their tunes with flair.

Bats make faces, swoop and dive,
While fireflies wink, oh so alive.
A rustle skirts the forest floor,
As pinecones tumble, laughter galore.

The tall trees nod, a jovial crowd,
Their knobby bark rings laughter loud.
In the twilight, joy's embrace,
Tickles the treetops, a merry chase.

So come, join in the whimsical twirl,
Under starlit maps, let laughter unfurl.
In dusky hues, let spirits rejoice,
Tickling hearts where nature's voice.

Revelations of Radiance in the Glade

In the glade, a bright surprise,
Sunbeams dance in youthful eyes.
Daisies whisper cheeky tales,
While honeybees take playful gales.

Beneath the boughs, a jolly sage,
Cracks jokes on a wooden stage.
With every chuckle, petals sway,
Frolicking laughter lightens the day.

Mushrooms cap'n a secret glee,
Winking at gophers, wild and free.
In this haven of riotous cheer,
Even the shadows can't hide their sneer.

So linger longer, let spirits flare,
In the glade where skits fill the air.
With rays of light, let joy cascade,
Revelations bright in the playful glade.

Mirthful Meandering Through Mossy Paths

Through mossy paths, a prank unfolds,
Tales of laughter, eager and bold.
Giggling ferns sway to a tune,
While shadows play beneath the moon.

With every step, a chuckle bursts,
As rabbits hop, oh how they thirst!
For little jokes and playful sights,
Tickled leaves on windy nights.

The ground itself joins in the jest,
As pebbles leap, they seem the best.
Nature's ribbons twine and twist,
Creating laughter, too hard to resist.

So roam these trails of whimsy and glee,
Let your heart dance, wild and free.
For in this walk, you'll truly find,
Mirthful meandering lingers behind.

Twinkling Eyes of Greener Pastures

In the meadow, cows wear hats,
The chickens dance, and tip their sprats.
A squirrel juggles acorns with flair,
While rabbits hop without a care.

The sunbeams tickle, laughter roams,
Underneath the leafy domes.
A fox plays tag with a wild hare,
In the bustling field, joy's everywhere.

A goat on stilts, a sight so grand,
He winks and nods, he's the best in the land.
The blues and greens, a playful twist,
In this pasture dance, none can resist.

As dusk approaches, shadows play,
The stars join in, a lively ballet.
With hearts alight, the night takes flight,
In this joyful place, everything feels right.

Mirage of Mirth in the Sylvan Haven

Beneath the trees, a picnic spread,
A laughter's echo, songs are fed.
The ants parade with crumbs in tow,
While chipmunks sing in a glorious show.

The wind whispers secrets, soft and light,
As fireflies wink and take to flight.
A wise old owl, with a comical stare,
Counts the stars from his humble lair.

In the thicket, a raccoon pranks,
Stealing snacks from laughing ranks.
The punchline waits in the rustling leaves,
Where joy is stitched in the fabric of eves.

As shadows stretch and daylight fades,
The forest giggles in playful parades.
With night's embrace, the tales ignite,
In this haven of mirth, hearts take flight.

Chuckling in the Canopy's Embrace

The trees are a stage for jesters bright,
With monkeys swinging, hearts take flight.
A parrot squawks a joke in vain,
While beetles dance in a merry train.

Beneath the boughs, a snail spins tales,
Of far-off lands and big fish fails.
A lizard nods, oh so wise,
With twinkling humor in his eyes.

Squirrels exchange their nutty looks,
While underfoot, the earthworm hooks.
With giggles shared in whispering leaves,
They spin their stories as evening weaves.

In the night, the stars join the fun,
With twinkling smiles, they all run.
In the canopy, laughter's lace,
Finds a home in nature's embrace.

Seductive Secrets of the Shadowed Woods

In the twilight's dance, the shadows tease,
Whispers float on the gentle breeze.
A rabbit prances, a mischievous flair,
With secrets spun in the evening air.

The badger plays hide and seek with the moss,
While clever foxes count the loss.
With twinkling eyes, they share a grin,
In this realm where giggles begin.

Amidst the ferns, a party unfolds,
With critters bopping like tales of old.
In moonlit laughter, the night outshines,
As laughter rolls like intertwined vines.

In shadows deep, the wild things sigh,
With every chuckle, the stars comply.
Here in the woods, where mischief plays,
Secrets and laughter fill the days.

Mirth Amidst Nature's Tapestry

Beneath the boughs, a squirrel prances,
With acorn hats, they take their chances.
The wind plays tricks, a feather flies,
As laughter rises with the skies.

A rabbit leaps, in jig and twist,
While birds join in, none can resist.
With every hop, each chirp brings cheer,
This merry scene, so bright, so clear.

A chipmunk dances, tail held high,
While butterflies flit, oh me, oh my!
The creek chuckles, a soft reply,
In jest with nature, we can't deny.

Gather now, the woodland throng,
In playful harmony, we belong.
Each leafy laugh, a joyous sound,
In nature's weave, love will abound.

The Playful Spirits of Evergreens

Amidst the pines, a prankster hides,
With shadows cast where mischief bides.
A wily fox, with gleaming eyes,
Plans silly tricks, a grand surprise.

The owls hoot in their sleep-filled glee,
As raccoons conspire near the tree.
With twigs and leaves, they craft their game,
In nature's realm, jesters proclaim.

The sunbeams wink through leafy seams,
Chasing the chipmunk's fleeting dreams.
With every rustle, giggles flow,
The forest's joy, a vibrant show.

A dance of sprites, the fairies' flight,
In moonlit glades, they twirl at night.
With laughter bright, they weave the air,
In playful twirls, free from care.

Antics in the Mossy Refuge

In twilight hues, the shadows play,
Moss carpets lush where critters sway.
A hedgehog rolls, a tumble, a spin,
As giggles echo, where fun doth begin.

The frogs croak tunes, a ribbiting band,
While fireflies twinkle, holding hands.
With every leap, a splash of cheer,
In this green haven, laughter draws near.

A squirrel juggles with acorn flair,
As brave little mice take to the air.
With every prank, the woods respond,
In this joyful nest, of nature fond.

The night takes shape, with sparkles bright,
As creatures whirl in pure delight.
An anthem of fun, a woodland jest,
In mossy refuge, we're truly blessed.

Chimes of Laughter in the Wooded Nest

In the wooded nook, where giggles grow,
The breezy whispers begin to flow.
A parrot squawks, a riddle rant,
While critters chuckle, all too gallant.

The sunbeams dance on leaves up high,
As playful shadows dart and fly.
With every rustle, a chuckle's born,
In nature's warmth, there's no need to mourn.

The owls hoot soft, in silly serenade,
While rabbit poses, a grand charade.
Sideways strut, a tiny deer,
In every heart, there's nothing to fear.

Gather 'round, let stories unfold,
In this lush realm, together, we're bold.
With joy as our guide, we'll roam and jest,
In the wooded nest, we are truly blessed.

Lively Legends of the Leafy Realm

In the grove where laughter thrives,
   Squirrels play with acorn dives.
Frogs wear hats, in grand parade,
   All the trees join in charade.

Breezes tickle leafy ears,
   Trees giggle, shedding fears.
Bumblebees hum silly tunes,
While raccoons dance under moons.

A wise old owl spins a tale,
Of cheeky mice, quite out of scale.
With tiny coats and shoes so bold,
   Their antics never grow old.

When the sunset paints the sky,
   Owls wink as they pass by.
In this realm where joy takes wing,
   Every creature's a comedian king.

The Sprightly Serenade of the Trees.

Beneath the boughs, a rooster sings,
Telling tales of magical flings.
The toads throw parties on the grass,
While fireflies illuminate the pass.

Every branch has a story, a jest,
From wise old oak to the curly crest.
Mice in trousers tap dance with flair,
As butterflies twirl in the warm air.

Laughing leaves sway, their giggles high,
Tickling the clouds way up in the sky.
A raccoon magician steals the show,
With a wink and a trick that makes hearts glow.

Amidst the fun and frolic they weave,
Nature's humor is hard to believe.
Each chuckle shared, each joke that's spun,
In this leafy realm, the joy can't be outdone.

Whispers Among the Twisted Pines

Twisted pines share quirky schemes,
As squirrels plot their nutty dreams.
Laughter echoes through the bark,
While shadows dance and leave a mark.

A tiny snail with a big top hat,
Claims he can outrun a playful cat.
Frogs leap forth with leaps so grand,
Creating rumbles across the land.

Whispers travel on the breeze,
While butterflies perform with ease.
Jokes get lost, but not the fun,
In this wood where time's undone.

As day gives way and stars appear,
All the creatures gather here.
Underneath the starry dome,
Every laugh feels like a home.

Laughter Beneath the Canopy

Underneath the leafy spread,
Bouncing bunnies giggle and tread.
Each bush reveals a secret game,
While chipmunks stake their silly claim.

The partridge dons a feathered crown,
Strutting round in a glorious gown.
The bushes rumble with delight,
As critters join in this wild night.

A hedgehog's riddle makes them grin,
As echoes weave and twine and spin.
Every leaf becomes a friend,
Where the laughter seems to blend.

When morning light breaks through the mist,
Creatures laugh and can't resist.
In this canopy of cheer,
Every chuckle's crystal clear.

Glee in the Green Enclave

In a nook where shadows play,
Laughter twirls without delay.
A squirrel dances, full of cheer,
While mice debate the finest beer.

A rabbit dons a silly hat,
With wiggles, he spins 'round like that.
The trees giggle in rustling tones,
As cheeky winds ruffle their cones.

Above, a crow cracks a wisecrack,
In this grove, there's no heart that lacks.
The flowers chuckle, wear a grin,
As butterflies flit and join in.

Joy bubbles up like fresh spring rain,
In playful antics, there's no disdain.
The sun dips low, but spirits soar,
In this enclave, who could ask for more?

Pranks at Dusk's Embrace

When day gives way to dusk so bright,
Critters gather for evening delight.
A fox pretends to trip and fall,
While friends all gather to have a ball.

A hare tosses pies with great glee,
Dough and filling fly with esprit.
A chorus of giggles fills the air,
As hedgehogs join the merry affair.

The moon peeks down with a wink so sly,
While birds plot games in the sky.
They snatch a worm and dangle it low,
As laughter rings and spirits glow.

With each chuckle, joy takes flight,
In these antics, all feels right.
When the stars finally start to gleam,
In pranks, they find the sweetest dream.

Chuckles Beneath the Verdant Arch

Beneath the arch of leafy green,
A merry band of friends is seen.
A turtle slips on a slickened stone,
Causing giggles that brightly shone.

A parrot squawks a joke so loud,
As frogs croak tunes to impress the crowd.
Together they weave a jesting tale,
While fireflies twinkle as lights in the pale.

A dandy deer strikes a comical pose,
And the clumsy bear trips on a rose.
Laughter dances upon the breeze,
Sprinkling joy like honeyed bees.

With each snicker, the world feels bright,
In shadows flickering, there's pure delight.
In this patch of mirth, life's better shared,
Chuckles beneath, where no hearts are bared.

Amusements in the Whispering Woods

In the woods where whispers freely roam,
Creatures gather, far from home.
A raccoon juggles acorns high,
And a wise owl can only sigh.

The dancing sprites weave in and out,
Creating laughter, stirring doubt.
A weasel slips, then strikes a pose,
As giggles erupt from all of those.

The breeze tells tales of funny schemes,
While foxes frolic in their dreams.
Each bark of laughter, a sweet refrain,
Echoes softly like gentle rain.

In this realm of humorous glee,
Every prank is a jubilee.
As twilight falls, the antics abound,
In these woods, pure joy is found.

A Symphony of Silly Shadows

In shadows long, the laughter grows,
A squirrel prances on his toes.
With acorns stacked, he claims his prize,
While birds above roll playful eyes.

The sunbeams giggle through the leaves,
As rustling whispers tease and weave.
A rabbit hops, a dance so spry,
While butterflies flit low and high.

The breeze hums tunes of silly songs,
Where everything feels right and wrong.
A fox slips past in silly chase,
That grinning grin upon his face.

In this mixed-up grove of cheer,
Funny tales will draw us near.
With every chuckle and delight,
The shadows swing from day to night.

Antics of the Arbor Allies

The wise old owl looks down with glee,
For shenanigans are plain to see.
A raccoon juggles nuts with flair,
While chattering squirrels fill the air.

The trees all shake with leafy laughs,
At the antics of their playful halves.
A hedgehog struts in mismatched socks,
As rabbits play their funny knocks.

Beneath the branches, laughter rings,
From all the woodland, joy it brings.
The fawns are leaping, full of jest,
In this delightful woodland fest.

Each critter knows the game we play,
With silly antics every day.
As twilight falls, the giggles soar,
Echoing through the forest floor.

Chuckles in the Cedar Shade

Beneath the branches, secrets shared,
Where joyful hearts are never scared.
The chipmunks scurry, quick and spry,
Cracking jokes as clouds drift by.

A merry band of woodland friends,
Join in the fun, where laughter blends.
A wise old turtle tells a tale,
Of silly mishaps on the trail.

The rabbits roll in fits of glee,
While dappled sunlight dances free.
A bear performs his wobbly waltz,
But stumbles, causing all the faults.

In this cool shade, the chuckles rise,
With mirth reflected in their eyes.
For every giggle and cheer they make,
Is woven into the laughter's wake.

The Dance of the Dappled Light

In dappled light, the fun begins,
With shapes that twist and turn like spins.
A puppy bounds with joyful barks,
As shadows play their funny arcs.

The breeze carries a ticklish tune,
As flowers sway beneath the moon.
A group of frogs joins in the fun,
With leaps and croaks, they dance as one.

The sun spills warmth on every side,
As critters bump and bounce with pride.
A hedgehog spins, a clumsy dash,
The laughter follows in a splash.

In this grove where joy ignites,
With every turn, the laughter bites.
A symphony of silvery rays,
In this radiant dance of sunny plays.

Banter Among the Elders of the Forest

Old Oak chuckles at the breeze,
While Maple giggles with such ease.
Birch tells tales of a squirrel's race,
As Pine rolls on, a comical face.

Laughter rings from each tall tree,
With promises of nuts and glee.
Cedar hums a funny tune,
While Spruce dances under the moon.

The rabbits pause to catch a sound,
As humor swirls all around.
Mushrooms nod in merry cheer,
In this woodland, joy is near.

All embrace the silly lore,
In nature's light, they laugh some more.
A giggling breeze that come and goes,
In the forest where the funny grows.

Joyous Revelations in the Leafy Sanctuary

Harlequin leaves in morning's light,
Dancing warmly, such pure delight.
The sunbeams wink with a playful grin,
As the day of laughter does begin.

The brook babbles of jolly pranks,
While frogs leap in their silly flanks.
With every ripple, giggles flow,
In the leafy sanctuary, moonlit glow.

Chirpy birds tell punchlines true,
While flowers bloom in colors new.
The trees sway with a gentle beat,
As humor fills the forest seat.

Every leaf a playful tease,
Sharing jokes with the buzzing bees.
In nature's play, all sorrows fade,
Joyous secrets in the shade.

Capers in the Enchanted Wild

Bouncing bunnies with wild pranks,
Jump and tumble in leafy ranks.
Foxes grin with clever glee,
In the enchanted wild, carefree.

A raccoon holds up a shiny prize,
While laughter dances 'neath the skies.
The owl hoots a witty remark,
As creatures gather 'round the park.

In playful chases, joy ignites,
Each caper shared through starry nights.
Squirrels chatter, weaving tales,
Of nutty treasures and silly trails.

While twinkling stars join in the fun,
The wild ignites when day is done.
With every caper, spirits rise,
In the enchanted wild, under the skies.

Whimsy in the Shadowed Retreat

In the cool shade where whispers play,
Lies a space where laughter stays.
Mossy carpets cushy and bright,
Embrace the whimsy of day and night.

A hedgehog twirls, a sight to behold,
As stories of old and new unfold.
With dragonflies flitting to and fro,
They all partake in the humorous flow.

Toadstools giggle beneath the trees,
While breezes carry secrets with ease.
Here, the shadows laugh and prance,
In the retreat, it's a woodland dance.

The warmth of mirth envelops all,
Resounding joy, a lovely call.
In every corner, friendship's light,
Whimsy grows, an endless flight.

Laughing Leaves and Dancing Shadows

In the branches, whispers play,
Leaves crackle with a giggling sway.
Shadows twirl in a playful dance,
Nature's jest in a leafy romance.

Squirrels prance with nuts in tow,
Bounding fast, stealing the show.
Each acorn tossed, a laughing cheer,
Resonates bright, for all to hear.

The breeze chuckles, a soft delight,
Tickling branches beneath the light.
A sunbeam winks, a wink in jest,
Nature's humor, we're truly blessed.

Even the rocks wear a knowing grin,
Mysteries wrapped in a cheeky spin.
In this grove, where laughter grows,
Joy is constant, and mischief flows.

Games of Light in the Woodland Realm

Sunshine sprinkles like playful dots,
Through the leaves, a game of spots.
Bouncing rays, a vibrant race,
Every corner, a new light space.

Crickets chirp their merry tunes,
Underneath the lazy moons.
Each note a laugh, a tease so sweet,
Nature's rhythm, a rhythmic feat.

A fox trips over hidden roots,
Fluffy tails in funny suits.
Chasing shadows, a breezy chase,
In the woodland, a lively place.

Beneath boughs of ancient lore,
Games of light we can't ignore.
With every giggle, and every gleam,
The forest weaves a funny dream.

Riddles of the Rustling Foliage

Whispers hidden in leafy folds,
Unraveling tales that nature holds.
Each rustle a riddle, a giggling game,
Inviting all to join the fame.

A wren fluffs up, with a cheeky tune,
Poking fun at the afternoon.
When leaves chuckle, the world aligns,
In this grove, where laughter shines.

Dancing petals in the gentle breeze,
Answer questions with playful ease.
Nature's jesters, wild and free,
Weaving joy for you and me.

As sunlight plays on twirling vines,
The riddle stings, but joy defines.
So step inside, embrace the cheer,
With rustling leaves, the fun is near.

Oddities Among the Shaded Shrubs

Beneath the bushes, sights are rare,
Mushrooms sport hats, a quirky flair.
A toadstool grins, so round and bold,
In the gloaming, a story told.

Pinecones giggle in the cool, soft shade,
Bouncing lightly, a merry cascade.
A hedgehog rolls, a spiky delight,
In the thicket, mischief takes flight.

Each blossom dons a curious face,
In this corner of nature's space.
Frogs leap high, as if to boast,
Among the shrubs, they play the host.

Oddities bloom where laughter's found,
In every rustle, a joyful sound.
So wander deep into this scene,
Where humor grows evergreen.

Revelry in the Aromatic Thicket

In shadows deep where laughter lies,
The trees wear smiles as daylight flies.
Beneath the boughs, a secret cheer,
With whispers bright that tickle the ear.

Squirrels dance on branches high,
While chipmunks wink as they dart by.
The breeze hums tunes from hearts so light,
As flowers giggle in pure delight.

A fox with flair sways to the beat,
While rabbits kick up their happy feet.
Each blossom bends to share a jest,
In this thicket where joy is blessed.

Here, the sun hops from leaf to leaf,
Sprinkling joy, dispelling grief.
In pockets of mirth, hear echoes ring,
Nature joins in, making hearts sing.

Tickles from the Woodland Spirits

Among the trunks, a giggle twirls,
Where mischief stirs and laughter swirls.
The misty air is laced with fun,
As sprites play tricks beneath the sun.

A deer stumbles, caught off guard,
While owls hoot loud, their laughs not hard.
Fairies flutter with sparkling eyes,
Proud of their tailored, clever lies.

In hidden glades, the shadows shout,
As ferns tiptoe, no fear, no doubt.
A feather floats with glittering grace,
Stirring up giggles in this place.

Mushrooms swirl like caps in jest,
Where trees erupt in joyful fest.
The woodland thrives, both bold and spry,
While friendly spirits laugh nearby.

Frolicking Fairies in the Leafy Realm

In patches green, where sunlight gleams,
Fairies weave their whimsical dreams.
They pirouette on petals bright,
Sowing giggles through day and night.

With tiny wands, they flick and wave,
Transforming twigs to pranks to save.
A butterfly bursts in laughter's dance,
Unraveling joy in each fleeting chance.

In every nook, mischief brews,
Where laughter's shade doth warmly ooze.
Sprites poke fun with glimmering eyes,
Crafting joy beneath the skies.

They ride the winds on dandelion seeds,
Unraveling tales that nature feeds.
In leafy realms, their wild spirits soar,
Leaving trails of fun at every door.

The Mischief of Nature's Keepers

Beneath the trees where secrets twine,
Nature's keepers conspire and shine.
With teasing tunes and playful plots,
They sow the mischief in magical spots.

A wise old owl with a twinkling eye,
Mocks the moon with a cheeky sigh.
A brook babbles jokes to rocks nearby,
As laughter ripples, soaring high.

With acorn hats and twiggy shoes,
Raccoons play tricks, spreading the news.
Leaves perform a merry jig,
In this woodland, both small and big.

Each rustling bush holds whispers deep,
Where laughter blooms and secrets creep.
In nature's realm, the jesters bloom,
Crafting joy to pierce the gloom.

Quirks of the Curious Quercus

In twisted trunks, the squirrels dance,
With acorns flying, it's their chance.
A grumpy owl with glasses round,
Says, "Who's making all this sound?"

The branch was weak, the winds were strong,
A raccoon sang a laundry song.
The leaves they tickled, laughter spread,
While sleepy ants rolled off to bed.

A ladybug wore polka dots,
And beetles clashed in silly plots.
Each tree has tales, each root a grin,
Nature's playground, let's begin!

The clouds above start drifting low,
A feathered mob with quite a show.
With flapping wings and chirps so clear,
They turn the woods into a sphere!

Echoes of Elation in the Elders

The ancient oaks, with branches wide,
Share secrets only they could guide.
A squirrel stirs, with chocolate stash,
While old pine grumbles, a giant clash!

The moonlit nights bring tales untold,
Of mischievous sprites and treasures bold.
An acorn's tale of dreams it spins,
Of epic journeys and silly grins.

From lofty heights, the views are grand,
The bunnies plot a giggle band.
With hops and skips, they dance about,
Their laughter echoes, free of doubt.

In every nook, a jest lies near,
A whisper, a chuckle, all sincere.
The winds embrace, the laughter swells,
In playful tales, the forest dwells.

Wink of the Wistful Willows

Beneath the willows, shadows play,
A cat with dreams of fishy bay.
It rolls and tumbles, lost in sleep,
While chirping crickets sing and leap.

A dandelion, dressed in gold,
Shares whispers of adventures bold.
With every breeze, the petals sway,
As if to smile and dance all day.

The rabbits wear their finest hats,
As they join in on jovial spats.
A picnic set with berries bright,
Turns into a food fight delight!

With laughter ringing through the trees,
Each gust a wink, a gentle tease.
The willows bow, a friendly jest,
In nature's humor, we are blessed.

Frothy Fables of the Forest Floor

On forest floors where mushrooms sprout,
A wise old turtle takes his route.
With berry stains and tales galore,
He chuckles at the raindrops' score.

A slinky snake, in shades so bright,
Practices moves in pure delight.
Each funny wiggle sets the scene,
A dance-off near the evergreen.

The frogs with crowns declare a game,
Who jumps the most shall earn the fame!
Among the ferns, the laughter grows,
With silly songs, in rows and rows.

The dappled sun beams down to share,
A whispered giggle through the air.
In every nook, the joy is stored,
With frothy fables to be adored!

Fleeting Moments of Joy in the Shade

Under leafy canopies, laughter sprouts,
Squirrels chase shadows, darting about.
A tale of twigs, a chorus of glee,
Nature's chuckles, wild and free.

A butterfly slips, a dance in the breeze,
Tickling the flowers, with such playful ease.
The sunbeams wink, bright prisms of light,
As giggles entwine with day and night.

A rabbit hops high, declares with a grin,
"Life is a joke, let's start to spin!"
The brook joins in with a bubbling laugh,
While trees sway gently, a verdant staff.

In this merry grove, all worries are thin,
The heart skips a beat, let the fun begin!
For in every whisper and soft rustle's cheer,
The joy of the moment is perfectly clear.

Capering Spirits Celebrating Nature

Among the branches, spritely forms prance,
With twirls and giggles, they join in a dance.
Each leaf a witness to their playful scheme,
As sunlight plays tag, a sweet, golden dream.

The crows crack jokes in caws loud and bold,
As shadows on earth weave stories untold.
A hedgehog pops up, all spines set to tease,
While crickets compose a symphony with ease.

Beneath the tall oaks, a party takes flight,
With mushrooms as tables for fungus delight.
The wildflowers applaud with colors so bright,
Celebrating nature's whimsical night.

With spirits alight, they spin tales of lore,
In a world of laughter, who could ask for more?
For every rustle reveals hidden delights,
In the heart of the forest, where joy ignites.

The Lighthearted Heart of the Forest

In the archway of branches, the heart beats loud,
With squirrels in tutus, they're feisty and proud.
A rustle, a giggle, oh what could it be?
The forest is alive, so wild and carefree.

A floppy-eared bunny wears glasses askew,
Critiquing the flowers, with a knowledgeable view.
The melt of the sun paints everything gold,
As secrets exchange that could never be told.

With acorns as hats, the jays take their stand,
Directing the fun, with a wing and a hand.
The breeze sings the songs only nature can make,
While laughter cascades like a bubbling lake.

Joy leaps through the glades, never to fade,
In the arms of this grove, all worries unmade.
For the heart of the forest, with humor so bright,
Is a sanctuary wrapped in pure, playful light.

Whirling Tales from the Wilderness

In dappled light, the stories twirl,
As critters conspire, giving fate a whirl.
A crow with a quip, a fox with a grin,
In the haven of green, the fun all begins.

With each step they take, the forest conspirators,
Unraveling tales like woodland narrators.
Underfoot, the leaves laugh, rustle and play,
As nature spins yarns that brighten the day.

A deer in a hat, quite dapper and neat,
Struts like royalty, the forest's elite.
With wildflowers giggling, they waft in the breeze,
While laughter resounds through the towering trees.

So gather the joy, let the whimsy unfold,
For in this vast wilderness, mirth is pure gold.
With each whirling tale, a spark is ignited,
In the heart of the wild, where spirits are delighted.

Boughs of Banter and Delight

In the shade of fabled trees,
Laughter dances with the breeze.
Squirrels chatter, jokes exchanged,
Every twig a tale arranged.

A bumblebee buzzes with style,
A rabbit hops, a playful guile.
The mushrooms giggle, what a sight,
Under the sun, everything's bright.

Chipmunks mimic every sound,
Echoes of joy all around.
A wise old owl, in a merry mood,
Shares his secrets, chuckles brewed.

Frogs leap in a jolly show,
With each splash, their spirits glow.
In this grove, where laughter's sown,
Every heart feels right at home.

The Whimsical Wind's Whistle

The wind arrives with a playful twist,
Carrying whispers that can't be missed.
Leaves giggle as they swirl and sway,
Branches bend in a merry ballet.

A raccoon grins, a hat on his head,
Wearing mischief as he's being led.
The brook chuckles with a bubbly voice,
In this frolic, we all rejoice.

An old tree trunk, a storyteller wise,
Shares wild tales under blushing skies.
With each line, the woodland cheers,
A carnival of fun through the years.

While shadows dance and twilight streaks,
Moonbeams join as the forest speaks.
In this grove, where smiles entwine,
Every creature feels divine.

Enchantment in the Enigmatic Underbrush

Among the ferns, where secrets hide,
Come playful creatures, side by side.
A hedgehog spins, a dizzying waltz,
While mischief sparks without a halt.

Mirthful mushrooms glow in rows,
Each plume a cap, where laughter grows.
The wise fox shares riddle and jest,
In this nook, all are at their best.

The flowers gossip, what a scene!
With buzzing bees, they twist and preen.
Every footstep, a tickled thrum,
In this haven, all hearts become.

With twilight's brush, the day does close,
But joy remains, as night bestows.
In underbrush where giggles dwell,
Life is a whimsical carousel.

Chortles from the Charmed Copse

In the copse, where chuckles rise,
Every branch holds sweet surprise.
A thrush bursts forth with glee-filled songs,
Nature's chorus righting wrongs.

Giggling grasses in a sunny mound,
Dancing lightly on merry ground.
A playful breeze tickles at play,
Whisking off worries of the day.

The cautious deer, with a curious glance,
Steps to join the woodland dance.
With every leap, the laughter leaps,
In this grove, joy forever keeps.

As night creeps in, the laughter fades,
Yet in the heart, the memory wades.
For in this copse, forever bright,
Lies the magic, pure delight.

Sunlit Smiles in the Shrubby Dell

In the dappled light they play,
Squirrels chitter and dance all day.
A catnap here, a bird's surprise,
Laughter sparkles, never dies.

A fox jumps high, a mischief's call,
Rolling down the grassy sprawl.
Beneath the branches, shadows sway,
Whispers of fun in bright display.

Children giggle, shadows twirl,
Mushroom caps in a silly whirl.
Tickles from the soft, warm breeze,
Joyful giggles float through the trees.

Every giggle, every cheer,
Echoes out for all to hear.
Nature's humor, wild and free,
Lives in every bumblebee.

Glee in the Glade of Gentle Breezes

Blades of grass like tickling fingers,
Bouncing joy that softly lingers.
Dancing flowers, bright and bold,
Whispers of secrets waiting to be told.

A frog leaps high with a splish and splash,
Grinning wide in a sudden flash.
Bees buzz in a merry race,
Chasing each other with a silly pace.

In the warm sun, shadows prance,
Swaying slow, they join the dance.
Tiny critters with laughter bright,
Spin and twirl in pure delight.

Moonlight glimmers, stars align,
Nature's giggle, a playful sign.
In every nook, find mirth anew,
While the world laughs right along with you.

The Riddles of the Rustling Leaves

Leaves that crackle, rustle, tease,
Nature's laughter floats on the breeze.
Secrets swish in every sound,
Where giggly whispers can be found.

A raccoon grins, a twig breaks loud,
Beneath the trees, a playful crowd.
They roll and tumble, each surprise,
With every twinkle in their eyes.

Squirrels chase in a hazel race,
Finding mischief in every place.
As shadows form in playful light,
Nature giggles into the night.

Each leaf a riddle, a joke or two,
Under the sun, laughter feels new.
So join the fun where the wild things weave,
Through the dance of the rustling leaves.

Revelations of the Rambunctious Roots

Roots that twist like silly jokes,
Whispering secrets of cheeky folks.
Beneath the soil, they scheme and plot,
Frogs and toads in a lively spot.

Jumping jacks on the ground so bright,
Bark that chuckles, oh what a sight!
Worms doing waltzes, kin so true,
Each wriggle brings a giggle or two.

Dancing shadows, spinning tales,
While gentle winds spread happy trails.
Twitching tails in the underbrush,
Bring the joy, make the laughter rush.

So heed the jests where the roots entwine,
In nature's realm, life's a fine line.
With every glance at nature's play,
You'll find a smile that's here to stay.

Loony Larks by the Singing Brook

A bird on a branch, oh what a sight,
Dancing and chirping, full of delight.
With a wiggle and wobble, it sings its tune,
Making the frogs croak their own little rune.

The brook bubbles up, tickling the toes,
Where splashes and giggles create silly shows.
Fishes all flip, doing tricks in the sun,
As laughter erupts, oh, what jovial fun!

Nearby, a squirrel with a nut in its mouth,
Tripping on roots as it scampers about.
It pauses, it ponders, then leaps with a cheer,
Creating a scene that draws everyone near.

In this realm of jest, where all come to play,
Nature's own comedy leads hearts astray.
With giggles and glee, it dances in rhyme,
Celebrating the merry moments of time.

Mischievous Murmurs of the Evergreen Grove

Whispers of pine, oh so sly and sweet,
Tickle the ears, making giggles repeat.
Creatures conspire behind each leafy screen,
Plotting their antics, a rascally scene.

A hedgehog rolls in, donning a hat,
While rabbits are laughing at that little spat.
Turbocharged turtles dash in a race,
With leaves for their flags, they pick up the pace.

The wind carries tales, both silly and bold,
Of acorns and pranks that never get old.
A squirrel drops acorns, creating a clatter,
As giggles ensue from the mischief and chatter.

In this grove of glee, all troubles seem small,
With laughter and joy, they invite one and all.
Each turn reveals wonders of merriment found,
Where funny mischief knows no bounds.

Fables Told by Flickering Fireflies

Round the firelight, stories take flight,
With fireflies glowing, dazzling at night.
Each tale they weave, with laughter entwined,
Of frogs in tuxedos, oh, aren't they refined?

A wise old owl, in spectacles round,
Tells jokes with a flair, where humor is found.
The crickets all chuckle, clapping their wings,
As the moon blushes softly, and joyfully sings.

Frolicking shadows, they dance upon leaves,
In playful communion, the nighttime achieves.
From misfit magpies, with hats on their heads,
To a spider in slippers that dances on threads.

In the warmth of the glow, fellowship thrives,
With giggles and stories, oh how laughter drives!
These fables of fun bring peace to the night,
In a world stitched together by humor's pure light.

Harmony of Chuckles in the Thicket

In the heart of the thicket, where shadows collide,
A chorus of chuckles runs wild, far and wide.
A raccoon with mischief sneaks up right behind,
Stealing your sandwich, oh, what a find!

With flutters of wings, the butterflies flit,
Spreading the gossip, they'll never just quit.
The deer start to giggle, their tails in a swish,
At the grumpy badger who grumbles, 'What's this?'

Here, jesters abound, both furry and sleek,
With pranks in the air, there's humor to seek.
A fox plays the fool, wearing socks on its paws,
In this captivating thicket where laughter just roars.

Together they frolic, this merry brigade,
Creating a spectacle, a comedic parade.
So join in the fun, let your worries take flight,
In the thicket of chuckles, we revel all night.

www.ingramcontent.com/pod-product-compliance
Lightning Source LLC
Chambersburg PA
CBHW071848160426
43209CB00003B/465